This book belongs to

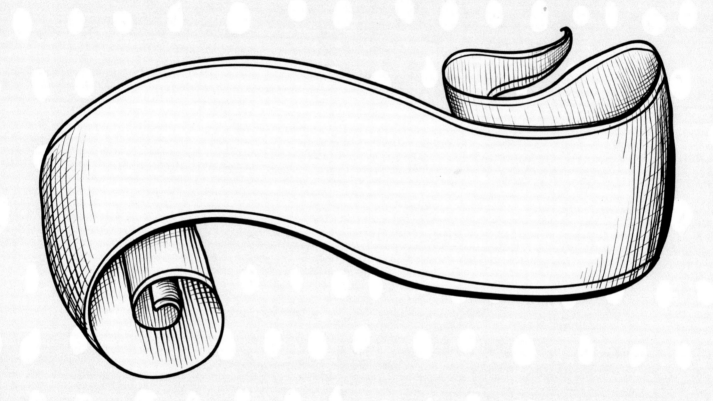

Many years ago, Jesus arrived on a donkey in Jerusalem. It was a Sunday. The people were very happy to see him. They waved palm branches to celebrate and laid them on the floor so the road wasn't too bumpy for the donkey.

We remember this day as Palm Sunday, which marks the start of Holy Week.

But not everyone loved Jesus.

"We need to get rid of Jesus. The people will follow him and not us," said Caiaphas, the high priest.

The other officials agreed. "He is claiming to be the Son of God. We do not believe him. We will lose all power if the people follow him," said one of the officials.

"Let's make a plan to get rid of Jesus," said Caiaphas the high priest.

The high priest and the officials came up with a plan to capture Jesus. They bribed Judas, who was one of Jesus' twelve disciples.

They gave Judas thirty silver coins in return for him leading them to Jesus.

Jesus knew his time on earth was coming to an end. He sat down for the last supper with his disciples. Jesus gave thanks for the food and broke the bread. "Eat; this is my body, which is broken for you," he said.

"One of you has betrayed me," said Jesus. The disciples were confused about who would do such a thing. Jesus knew it was Judas. After they ate, they drank the wine. The wine represented Jesus' blood, which was shed for mankind.

"Jesus, I promise to always stand next to you. I would lay down my life for you," said Peter. **Jesus knew that Peter would deny him.**

"I tell you, Peter, the rooster will not crow today until you deny that you know me three times," said Jesus.

"Let's go to the Garden of Gethsemane. I need to pray for strength," Jesus said to his disciples.

While he was praying, they had fallen asleep.

"Are you still sleeping? Look, the hour is near. My betrayer is approaching!" Jesus said.

Just then, a large crowd armed with weapons arrived, which had been sent by the chief priests and guided by Judas.

They arrested Jesus. He did not run; he willingly gave himself. They led him away.

Peter followed them at a distance. He waited outside. People started to recognize him as one of Jesus' followers. **When they asked Peter if he knew Jesus, he denied it.** He was scared to admit he was Jesus' disciple. "You are one of the twelve disciples!" shouted a man.

"I do not know or even understand what you are talking about," replied Peter. **He heard the rooster crow.** He remembered what Jesus had said. **He felt a rush of sadness and he began to cry out loud.**

During the time of Passover, it was custom for the Roman governor to release one Jewish prisoner chosen by the people. Pontius Pilate was the governor at the time. Pilate asked the crowd, "**Who should we keep as a prisoner? The notorious Barabbas or Jesus?**"

The high priests and officials had already spoken to the crowd and convinced them that Jesus was bad news.

"Jesus, Jesus!" the crowd shouted. "Crucify him! Crucify him!"
"What crime has he committed?" asked Pilate.
The crowd continued to shout louder.
Pilate realized he would get nowhere. He took some water and washed his hands, to show everyone that he did not want to be blamed for anything. This is where the phrase "washing our hands of something" comes from.

Jesus was beaten by the governor's soldiers, and a crown made of thorns was rammed onto his head. **He was forced to carry the cross through the streets of Jerusalem.**

The crowd laughed and mocked him. "All hail the king of the Jews," laughed a man.

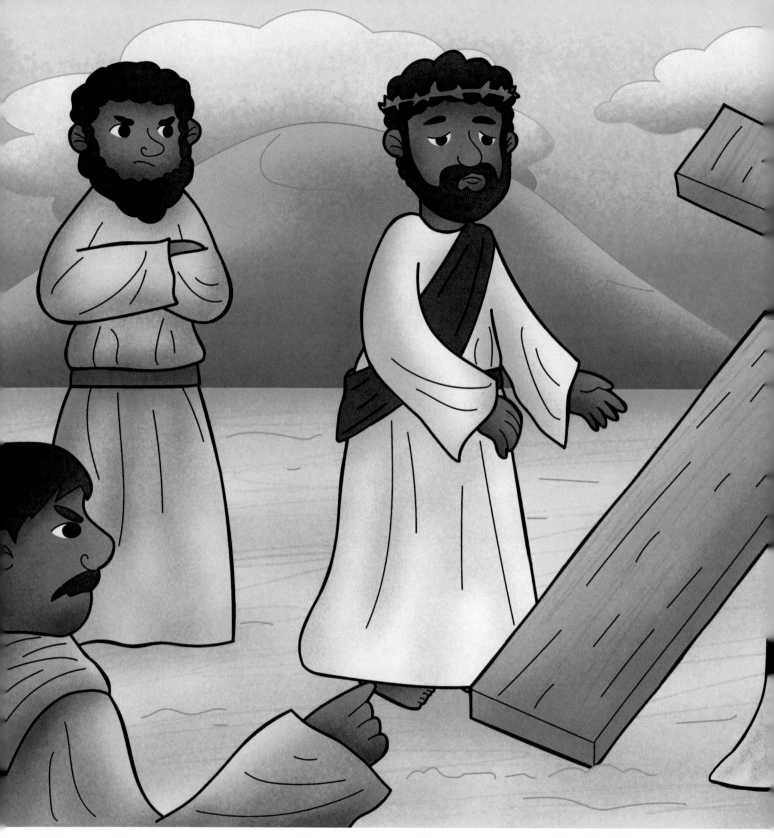

Jesus became too weak to carry the cross to the hill.

The soldiers took a bystander from the crowd called Simon. He was ordered to carry the cross for Jesus.

Jesus was on the cross at Golgotha for six hours before he died. Even though it was daytime, a darkness covered the whole land. It was a very sad time for humanity.

"Father, forgive them, for they don't know what they are doing," said Jesus as he prayed before his death.

Meanwhile, the veil of the temple was torn in two as Jesus died.

This thick, heavy curtain was used to separate the rest of the temple from the Holy of Holies, where the Ark of the Covenant was. Once a year, the high priest would visit and offer atonement for the sins of the people.

God was showing the people that they did not need to go through another person or ritual to reach Him.

The day after Jesus died was the Sabbath, the Jewish holy day. The Jewish leaders did not want the bodies left on the crosses. **Joseph of Arimathea was a respected member of the council who was said to be a secret follower of Jesus.** He got permission from Governor Pilate to bury Jesus. He and another council member, Nicodemus, wrapped Jesus' body in cloth.

Joseph owned a garden that had an unused tomb, and they placed his body in this tomb. The Romans had a guard watch over it. The Jewish leaders made sure the tomb was impossible to enter.

Early on Sunday morning, Mary Magdalene and some other women went to the tomb to put herbs on the body.

To their surprise, the stone had been rolled away, and Jesus was not there.

"Don't be amazed," said an angel. "You seek Jesus, the Nazarene, who has been crucified. **Jesus has risen.** He is not here. Behold the place where they laid him!"
The women were shocked and ran as fast as they could to tell the other disciples.

It had been forty days since Jesus had risen. He was in Bethany with his followers, and he prayed for them. Suddenly, the sky turned white, and a large shining cloud covered Jesus. "Soon, you will receive the power of the Holy Spirit. Tell my story to the people all over the world. I will see you all again someday," said Jesus.

Jesus was carried back into heaven, where he took his seat at the right hand side of God. With the power of the Holy Spirit, his disciples were able to speak many languages. They were able to spread Jesus' message quickly. Many became Christians that very day. **People continue to speak about Jesus and the sacrifices he made for mankind.**

If you have enjoyed this book, please leave a review on Amazon.
It has a significant impact on independent creatives like myself.
Thank you so much!

Jayla

Made in the USA
Coppell, TX
13 April 2022

76495771R00024